Oregon's Best Jokes

Elliot Maxx & Friends

All the people and events mentioned in this book are either the product of the author's imagination or are used in a purely fictional manner. In other words, they're just jokes. So lighten up, okay?

Oregon's Best Jokes

Copyright 1995 by Elliot Maxx

ISBN: 0-935735-03-8

All rights reserved

CONTRIBUTORS

Thanks to all of the people who contributed their jokes and feedback.

Joe Larson, Larry Pendergast, Dan Deprez, Steve Wilson, Darryl and Linda Igelmund, Stu Stuart, Steve Pendergast, Dwight Slade, Ed Newcomer, Robert Jenkins, Ron Reid, Bill and Donna Richards, Laura Crocker, Michelle Beaudry, Lonnie Bruhn, Art Krug, Laura, Megan & Emily Larson, Doug White, Tim Gallagher, Betty Holman, Kermet Apio, Ric Schrader, Ichabod Caine, Maria Cuenca, Heather Cullen, Erica Nelson, and Sadie.

And an extra special thanks to
GENE OPENSHAW
A good friend and a very funny man, who wrote a lot of the best material.

Contents

PORTLAND	7
THE BURBS	21
LAKE OSWEGO	27
SALEM	31
ALBANY	39
EUGENE	43
ROSEBURG	49
MEDFORD	53
ASHLAND	57
DUCKS & BEAVERS	61
THE COAST	67
EASTERN OREGON	73
OUTDOOR LIFE	79
OREGON NAMES	87

Portland

*A Rose By Any Other Name
Wouldn't Be As Soggy.*

What do you call two days of rain in Portland?
    A weekend.

*

What do you call three weeks of rain?
    The Rose Festival.

*

What did the Oregonian say to the Pillsbury Doughboy?
    "Nice Tan."

Portland

Did you know that, according to the statistics, it only rains about a dozen times a year in Portland?
January, February, March ...

*

A farmer from Eastern Oregon was telling his friend about his recent sightseeing trip to Portland.
"I enjoyed the Harbor Tour," said the farmer, "but I sure got wet."
"Really," said his friend. "I thought those boats were covered."
"Boats?" said the farmer. "What boats?"

*

What's the most popular sight to see in downtown Portland?
An empty parking space.

Oregon's Best Jokes

A guy from Paris, while on a sightseeing tour of downtown Portland, was completely unimpressed by everything he saw.

"Hah," said the Frenchman, "Your Convention Center is not so great. Our Eiffel Tower eez much bigger."

Next they went to the Portland Art Museum.

"Hah," the Frenchman went on, "In France, we have the Louvre, which eez also much bigger."

Finally, as they walked by the Salmon Street Springs Fountain, the Frenchman stopped in his tracks.

"I really must hand eet to your American technology," he said. "You don't know much about towers or museums, but you make a bidet that eez truly *formidable*."

Portland

Why do Portland commuters like to ride the Light Rail?
    It's a third less calories than the regular rail.

*

What's ruder than having a waiter at Jakes give you the razzberry?
    Having the chef at Benihana's give you the finger.

*

What do they call the birds that hang around Starbucks?
    The Swallows of Capuccino.

*

What's the difference between Starbucks and regular coffee?
    About two bucks a cup.

Oregon's Best Jokes

Meteorological experts predicted a massive flood that would destroy the world.

The Pope went on worldwide TV and said, "This is a punishment from God. Prepare to meet your maker."

The President went on TV and announced, "Our scientists have done all they can. The end is near."

The mayor of Portland came on and said, "Due to inclement weather, this year's Rose Festival will be moved to the top of Mount Hood."

*

How does a financial advisor from Southeast Portland diversify his portfolio?

He puts his money in both Megabucks and Powerball.

Portland

A downtown policeman finds a rather bedraggled looking man sprawled across a bench in front of the KOIN Tower.

"Hey, buddy. You can't sleep here," says the cop.

The man says nothing, just lets out a long, "Aaaaaaghghgh."

"Come on," the cop continues, "you know the law. If you don't move I'm gonna have to book you for loitering."

Still the man just goes, "Aaaaghggh."

"Okay, that's it," says the cop as he yanks the man to his feet. "You're under arrest. Where'd you come from, anyway?"

The man slowly points to the sky and wheezes, "Observation Deck."

Oregon's Best Jokes

How can you tell you're really in Portland?
    When you call 911 and they put you on hold.

*

In Portland, what's the difference between 911 and Domino's.
    When you call Domino's, they usually show up in 30 minutes or less.

*

Did you hear about the Portland Police Department's new survival training course?
    They drop you in the middle of a strange, crime-infested area and give you two hours to find the nearest Dennys.

Portland

How can you tell your car needs a tune-up?
    When you're downtown and you actually get pulled over by one of those cops on bikes.

*

What's more embarrassing than getting arrested by a cop on a bike?
    Having to ride to the station on the handlebars.

*

A cop stops a wino staggering along Burnside, "I think you're a little drunk today, pal. Didja know you got one foot in the gutter and one on the sidewalk?"

"Oh, thank God," says the drunk, "I thought I was going lame."

Oregon's Best Jokes

What's gray and white and flops around Old Town?
    A wino and a pigeon fighting over a cigaret butt.

*

One night, when an old derelict showed up drunk at a treatment center, the exasperated counselor said, "Ed, this is the fifteenth time we've dried you out. After all of that effort, you just keep drinking. How do you explain that?"
    "I dunno," shrugged the old wino, "tenacity?"

*

What do you get after four years of dope smoking?
    A degree from Reed College.

Portland

"Excuse me, pal. Could you spare five bucks for an espresso?"

Who is Portland's favorite rapper?
　Ice Latte'.

*

Why are the garbage rates so low in North Portland?
　　They gift-wrap their trash and let the kids steal it.

Oregon's Best Jokes

How do you keep from getting robbed in North Portland?
    Move.

*

How many straight Hawthorne District waiters does it take to screw in a lightbulb?
    Both of them.

*

Did you hear about the new Hawthorne District mafia?
    With the "kiss of death" you also get dinner and dancing.

*

Did you hear about Gus Van Sant's new film about life on 82nd Avenue?
    Even Call Girls Get The Blues.

Portland

An 82nd Avenue hooker goes into a bank to get change for a twenty.

"I'm sorry, ma'am," says the teller, "but this bill is counterfeit."

"Oh my god!" exclaims the hooker, "I've been raped!"

*

How many Sellwood antique dealers does it take to screw in a lightbulb?

Three. One to screw it in and the others to reminisce about how good the old bulb was.

*

Why is "The Oregonian" like a Portland Trailblazer Cheerleader?

Not very deep, but a great sports section.

Oregon's Best Jokes

What do you get when you cross a Trailblazer with a groundhog?
    Six more weeks of basketball season.

*

What do Trailblazer Cheerleaders and cowchips have in common?
    The older they get, the easier they are to pick up.

*

When an old lady asked a guide at the Washington Park Zoo why she couldn't find the elephants, he explained, "During mating season, ma'am, we keep them in the barn."
    "Do you think they would come out for peanuts?" she asked.
    "Lady," he said, "would you?"

Portland

One day at the Weinhardt Brewery, an employee was killed. The manager went to the widow's home to break the news.

"I'm sorry, ma'am," he said, "but your husband drowned in a vat of beer."

"Oh my god," gasped the widow. "Did he suffer much?"

"I don't think so," replied the manager. "He got out three times to take a leak."

The Burbs

VINI VIDI VEGGIE
I came, I saw, I landscaped.

What do you call an afternoon spent washing the car, trimming the hedge and mowing the lawn?
 The Hillsboro Triathalon.

*

What's the difference between Beaverton and Hillsboro?
 In Beaverton, they're worried about having a BMW. In Hillsdale, they're just worried about having a BM.

The Burbs

For a Beaverton housewife, what makes time stand still?
 Her twenty-ninth birthday.

*

Did you hear about the new bank in Oregon City?
 You bring in a toaster and they give you $10,000.

*

In Beaverton, they say: It's 10 o'clock -- do you know where your children are?
 In Gresham, they say: It's 10 o'clock -- do you know *who* your children are?
 In Troutdale, they say: It's 10 o'clock -- do you know what time it is?

Oregon's Best Jokes

Two tourists see the Tualatin exit on I-5. The wife says, "Let's stop in Toooalatin."
"It's *Twa*latin," says the husband.
"*Tooo*walatin," repeats the wife.
"It's *Twa*latin."
After a few minutes they decide to stop and ask. They go into the first place they see and the husband says to the kid at the counter, "Okay kid, real slow and real distinctly -- where are we?"
The kid says, "Daaaaaaay-reeeee Queeeeeeeeeeen."

*

What's the hardest part of putting on a Christmas Pageant in Gresham?
Trying to find three wise men and a virgin.

The Burbs

What do you wear to a Milwaukie wedding?
    Formal Bowling Shirts.

*

What is Forest Grove's idea of a psychedelic experience?
    Alzheimer's.

*

Why doesn't anyone from Tigard ever win the Portland Marathon?
    They keep stopping to ask for Directions.

*

Why don't they snort cocaine in Tualatin?
    It keeps sliding off the bathroom mirror.

Oregon's Best Jokes

When do Vancouver women look their best?
    At two minutes to closing.

*

What's the difference between Vancouver and yogurt?
    Yogurt has culture.

*

What is the most popular form of contraception in Milwaukie?
    Keeping your underpants on.

*

Why don't they drink Kool-Aid in Wilsonville?
    No one knows how to get a quart of liquid in the little package.

The Burbs

Why don't Tigard women use birth control pills?
> They keep falling out.

*

How can you tell that your secretary is from Gresham?
> She's got Wite-Out all over her computor screen.

*

What do you call a biker from Wilsonwille?
> Rebel Without A Clue.

*

What's green, red, purple, orange, pink and covered with polka dots?
> A lady from Troutdale dressed up for church.

Lake Oswego

Walden Pond with an attitude

What's 911 in Lake Oswego?
The Porsche Hotline.

*

What's the Lake Oswego version of a Pit Bull fight?
Two poodles yapping at each other until one of them wets the carpet.

Page 27

Lake Oswego

What do they mean by "quality time" in Lake Oswego?
Thinking about your kids while you're golfing.

*

What's a stable family environment in Lake Oswego?
Having the same babysitter every night.

*

Todd was backing out of the driveway when he crashed into his neighbor's new Mercedes.
"What am I going to tell him?" he cried. "I just ran over his new car!"
"Better break it to him gently," advised Todd's wife. "First, tell him it was one of the kids."

Oregon's Best Jokes

Lake Oswego Mom's Cookbook

What's a Lake Oswego housewife's favorite thing to make for dinner?
    Reservations.

*

How does a Lake Oswego mom call her family for dinner?
    "Come on, kids. Get in the car."

Lake Oswego

What kind of containers do Lake Oswego housewives use to store leftovers?
Yupperware.

*

What kind of laundry whitener do they use in Lake Oswego?
Nouveau Bleache.

*

What do you call black people in Lake Oswego?
Trailblazers.

*

At a daycare class, how can you tell which baby is from Lake Oswego?
The one with the Pampers tied around his neck.

Salem

"Election? I thought you said ..."

A young woman was applying for a job as Senator Packwood's new secretary.

After the initial interview was over, he said, "You know, you are the third person today to claim that I sexually harassed them during this interview."

"But Senator," replied the young applicant, "I haven't been sexually harassed."

"True," said the Senator. "But you haven't finished the interview yet, either."

Salem

What did Senator Packwood give his staff for the holidays?
 A Christmas goose.

*

If Sleeping Beauty lived in Salem, what would Prince Charming be?
 Under investigation.

*

How many Oregon Senators does it take to screw in a lightbulb?
 "I didn't screw anybody."

*

What was the first indication that Senator Packwood might be guilty of sexual misconduct?
 He didn't know "harass" was one word.

Oregon's Best Jokes

What do Bob Packwood and Bob Vila have in common?
    They're both pretty handy.

*

Did you hear about Packwood's new peace demonstration?
    "Hands Across My Secretary."

*

Did you hear about Senator Packwood's new self-help book?
    "How to Win Back the Friends You've Already Influenced."

*

What do you get when you cross Bob Packwood with a proctologist?
    A politician who wants to kiss your ass.

Salem

What do an honest politician and Bigfoot have in common?

Nobody has ever seen one.

*

Two women run into one another at the Supermarket and begin talking about their children.

"So, how is your oldest son?" asks Betty.

"He's doing fine," replies Marge. "He's a successful engineer with a beautiful wife, three great kids and a gorgeous home in Lake Oswego."

"That's nice," says Betty. "And how's your youngest son, the mentally retarded boy?"

"Oh," says Marge, "he's doing fine, too. In fact, it looks like he might even get re-elected."

Oregon's Best Jokes

**Caution
State Legislature in Session**

What's the worst thing about local political jokes?
    Some of them get elected.

*

What's the difference between an Oregon Legislator and a jellyfish?
    A jellyfish is *born* spineless.

Salem

Governor Kitzhaber was speaking to a group of Indians at the Warm Springs Reservation.

When he promised better schools, they shouted, "Umpqua! Umpqua!"

When he promised them better living conditions, again they shouted, "Umpqua! Umpqua!"

When he promised they could count on the government for trust and brotherhood, the crowd jumped to their feet and began to chant, "Umpqua! Umpqua! Umpqua!"

Overwhelmed by their response, Kitzhaber asked one of the tribal elders for a tour of the reservation.

"Okay, but be careful," said the chief. "We keep a few horses out here. I wouldn't want you to step in any of the umpqua."

Oregon's Best Jokes

After one of Senator Hatfield's press conferences, a tired reporter returned to the newsroom.
"Long speech," said the editor.
"Sure was," said the reporter.
"What was it about?"
"I don't know," replied the reporter. "He didn't say."

*

How can you tell when it's winter in Salem?
The politicians have their hands in their own pockets.

*

What's the difference between armed robbery and Oregon's state income tax?
The gun.

Salem

What's the difference between the State Legislature and the Ringling Brothers Circus?
    At Ringling Brothers, no one takes the clowns seriously.

*

What's the difference between the State Legislature and a 4-H Exhibit at the Oregon State Fair?
    The 4-H exhibit is only full of crap for three months of the year.

*

How many Oregon activists does it take to screw in a lightbulb?
    Five. One to screw it in and four to file the environmental impact statement.

Albany

Smell's Half Acre

What do you call a Sasquatch in Albany?
    Bigfart.

*

What is Albany's favorite Mexican Holiday?
    Stinko de Mayo.

*

What do Campbell's Soup and Albany's air have in common?
    They're both "so thick you can eat 'em with a fork."

Albany

Why does Albany smell?
    So that blind people can hate living there, too.

*

The smell from Albany's so rude
It made one young tourist conclude
The cause of the scent
Came from each resident
Eating too darn much Mexican food.

*

Did you hear about President Clinton's visit to Albany?
    He didn't inhale.

*

Did you hear about Albany's new Scratch-n-Sniff Lottery?
    If it smells like crap, you lose.

Oregon's Best Jokes

**Official Seal of The
Albany Chamber of Commerce**

Why is it impossible to walk across Albany?
> No one can hold their breath that long.

*

What do they call Albany's three day celebration of painting, crafts and music?
> Fartquake.

Albany

A guy from Portland, a guy from Eugene and a guy from Albany were walking past a foul smelling pigsty at the Oregon State Fair. They decided to make a bet on who could stay inside the longest.

After five minutes, the guy from Portland came out.

After ten minutes, the guy from Eugene came out.

After twenty minutes, the pigs came out.

Eugene

Friends Don't Let Friends Drive Volkswagens

What do you call a Eugene "Rennaisance Man?"
> A guy who can smoke pot, read your aura, and play air guitar at the same time.

*

What's the difference between a sasquatch and a hippie chick from Eugene?
> No matter how loaded you get a sasquatch, he won't dance in front of the stage at a Grateful Dead concert.

Eugene

How can you spot a seagull from Eugene?
    It's got hair under its wings.

*

What's the difference between the Eugene Saturday Market and a farm auction?
    At a farm auction, the cows rarely wear paisley dresses?

*

How do you handle a labor dispute in Eugene?
    Transcendental Mediation.

*

Did you hear about Eugene's new remedial Palm Reading Course?
    It's called *Hooked on Fingers*.

Oregon's Best Jokes

A guy from Eugene was searching for the meaning of life. Hoping to find the answer, he sold everything and travelled to India to seek out the Maharishi Maghesh Yogi.

When he got there, he was brought to a room filled with candles. In the center of the room sat the old mystic in a deep trance.

"Master," said the young man, "I have come thousands of miles. What is the meaning of life?"

"Life," said the old man, opening one eye, "is a river."

The young man waited in silence, but the Maharishi said nothing more. Finally the young man asked, "What do you mean, 'Life is a river?'"

"All right," shrugged the guru, "life is *not* a river."

Eugene

"Woodstock was beautiful, man. I slept in a ditch for three days."

A hippie chick was standing at a bus stop in Eugene with her breast hanging out of her blouse.

A cop pulled up and said, "Hey, lady! I don't know what you think you're doing, but this is really out of line — even for Eugene!"

"Oh my god!" she exclaimed, looking down at her open blouse. "I left the baby on the bus!"

Oregon's Best Jokes

A shriveled, elderly hippie was sitting contentedly on a bench at the Eugene Saturday Market when a young woman walked by.

Amazed by the serene look on his face, she said, "You look like you don't have a care in the world."

"I don't," said the frail, old man.

"Really?" she said. "What is the secret of your happiness?"

"Well," said the old man, rubbing his gray whiskers, "I have spent my life following the Grateful Dead, wherever they performed, drinking, partying, taking drugs and sleeping in my van."

"That's incredible!" exclaimed the young woman. "And just how old are you?"

"Twenty-three."

Eugene

What the newest department store in Eugene?
> The Bong Marche'.

*

How many Deadheads does it take to screw in a lightbulb?
> None. Deadheads don't screw in lightbulbs. They screw in the back of Volkswagen Vans.

*

Why are people from Eugene so unimpressed with astroturf?
> Most of the folks there have been growing grass indoors for years.

Roseburg

If a tree falls in the woods and no one's there to hear it, who cares?

What do you get when a Spotted Owl sees its shadow?
>Six more weeks of unemployment.

*

If Paul Bunyon lived in Roseburg, what would he be?
>Out of work.

Roseburg

The first day at a lumber camp, Bob went out to try his hand at cutting down a tree.

He stopped by the tool shed to check out a saw.

"I recommend this chainsaw," said the tool clerk. "It can cut down fifty trees a day."

That night, Bob came back and complained, "This saw only cut down three trees, today. I think it must be broken."

"Well, let me have a look at it," replied the tool clerk.

Bob handed him the chainsaw. The clerk set it on the ground, gave the cord a yank and the saw roared to a start.

"Hey!" shouted Bob. "What's that noise?"

Oregon's Best Jokes

"I don't like to look at it as unemployment. I prefer to think of it as a blue-collar sabbatical."

What do you call it when a Spotted Owl poops in the forest?
  Endangered feces.

*

What's the latest creature added to the endangered species list?
  Oregon loggers.

Roseburg

What's the difference between Roseburg and poverty?
>You can get used to living in poverty.

*

Why do Roseburg tavern owners save their empty beer bottles?
>For their customers who don't drink.

Medford

Klan Of The Cave Bear

Why do so many guys from Medford drive 4x4's?
> It reminds 'em of the last math equation they ever solved.

*

What's the hardest part about being a yuppie in Medford?
> Getting the gunrack to fit in your BMW.

Medford

A young couple moved to Medford. As they were unpacking their belongings, a neighbor walked by and said, "Excuse me. You people ain't liberals, are you?"

"Why do you ask?" inquired the young man.

"Well," said the neighbor, "Medford is a very conservative community, and we wouldn't want you young folks stirring up trouble."

"What do you mean by conservative?" asked the young man.

"For one thing," said the neighbor, "almost 90% of the people here voted for Reagan."

"So what?" replied the young man. "A lot of people voted for Reagan."

"Last year?" said the neighbor.

Oregon's Best Jokes

What's "integration" in Medford?
    Hosting a foreign exchange student from Canada.

*

What's a Medford *mixed marriage?*
    Getting hitched to someone outside of your immediate family.

*

What's the most dangerous part of being a Medford bigot?
    Lighting a cross on someone's lawn during a burn ban.

*

Where do Medford bigots buy their sheets?
    KKK Mart.

Medford

What do you get when you cross a white supremacist with a stock broker?
    A Merrill Lynching.

*

What's the definition of "politically correct" in Medford?
    Equal opportunity for all white Anglo-Saxon Protestants -- regardless of their race, creed or color.

Ashland

*To be or not to be --
What kinda question is that?*

The world-famous Elizabethan Theatre opened a recent season with a terrible production of Hamlet.

It was a tense time for everyone involved. On opening night, the cast was backstage fighting and bickering among themselves.

When the director walked in and saw them, he said, "You people are acting very badly."

"Oh yeah?" replied one of the cast. "Well, you're not directing that well , either."

Ashland

A famous director from New York came to Ashland to direct Romeo and Juliet. The actors were having a difficult time with one of the big fight scenes and finally the director threw down the script in frustration.

"What's the matter with you people?" he screamed, "Haven't you ever done any stunt work before?"

"No," replied one of the actors.

"Well, it's not that difficult," said the director, grabbing a fencing sword. "Now watch."

And with that, the director jumped up on stage. He fought off several attacks from the other actors, dove through a window and then lunged from a balcony to the stage twenty feet below.

Oregon's Best Jokes

"That," he said to the actors, "is how it is done in New York! Now, everybody in your places and let's try it again!"

"Yes sir," said the actors.

"Oh, and one other thing," said the director. "Somebody call an ambulance -- I think I broke my leg."

*

A young man sat down next to a pretty young lady on the bus to Ashland.

"My name's Bill," said the young man. "What's yours?"

"Linda." replied the young lady.

"What do you do around here?"

"I'm an actress."

"Really?" said the young man. "Which restaurant?"

Ashland

What do you get when you cross a bad Shakespearean actor with a mafia boss?
    An offer you can't understand.

*

What does Ashland call a third-rate actor from New York?
    A star.

*

A young actor from a small town in Eastern Oregon decided to try his luck in Ashland.

After a thoroughly embarrassing audition, the director asked him, "Son, have you ever read Shakespeare before?"

"I don't know," said the kid. "Who wrote it?"

Ducks and Beavers

Land of the Macho Mascots

Top Ten Alternative Oregon University Mascots
1. The Prancin Poodles of the Pac-10
2. The Fighting Amish
3. Weiner Dogs From Hell
4. Four Ponies of the Apocalypse
5. The Oregon State Stormin Sycophants
6. The University of Oregon Grapes
7. The Fighting Ferns of OSU
8. The Oregon State Slugs
9. The Corvallis Caterpillers
10. The Eugene Eunuchs

Ducks & Beavers

During summer vacation, the Beaver's Head Coach noticed a young fellow on a farm in Prineville running after some livestock.

The boy showed great speed and agility as he darted back and forth, herding the animals into the barn.

The coach was so impressed, he stopped his car and called to the young farmer, "Son, I am very impressed with your athletic ability."

"Gosh, thanks," said the farmer.

"I think you would make one heck of a fine football player," the Coach added, handing him a football. "Here, son. Do you think you could pass this thing?"

"Pass it?" replied the player. "Gee, Mister, I don't even think I could swallow it."

Oregon's Best Jokes

What's the difference between the Beavers and the Ducks?
>About 14 points a game.

*

At OSU, what's the difference between a beaver and a pig?
>The beaver is the mascot. The pig is the homecoming queen.

*

Why does the Beaver Marching Band play during halftime?
>To keep the cheerleaders from grazing.

*

How do you check a Beaver Cheerleader's I.Q.?
>With a tire gauge.

Ducks & Beavers

What has enormous boobs and stands on the sidelines?
    The OSU Coaching Staff.

*

Why do the Beaver Cheerleaders wear earplugs?
    To keep their heads from deflating.

*

What has 8 legs and an I.Q. of 50?
    Four Oregon Alumni watching the Rose Bowl.

*

Why did the Duck Cheerleader have rectangular boobs?
    She forgot to take the tissue out of the box.

Oregon's Best Jokes

"Okay, men -- no mistakes. If we receive, recover that fumble. And if we kickoff, hang in there and block that extra point."

What keeps the Beavers from going to the Rose Bowl?
    The other teams.

Ducks & Beavers

How many Beavers does it take to screw in a light bulb?
    Two. One to screw it in and the other to recover the fumble.

*

What's the most popular frathouse at the University of Oregon?
    Phi Beta Keggar.

*

What's the first sign you might have a drinking problem at the University of Oregon?
    When your blood-alcohol level surpasses your grade-point average.

The Coast

Where a Day Without Sunshine is Like Nine Months of the Year.

A California tourist called the Brookings Visitor's Bureau, "Does it really rain as much as they say?"

"Yes, I'm afraid so," replied the receptionist. "Last year, we got more than thirty inches of rain in less than three months!"

"Wow," said the tourist. "Winter must be pretty rough up there."

"Winter?" said the receptionist. "Heck, that was last summer!"

The Coast

Crab Fishing in Astoria

What's Scandinavian and has an I.Q. of 140?
    Astoria.

*

How do they make sushi in Astoria?
Tuna fish and minute rice.

Oregon's Best Jokes

An old fisherman walked into a store and ordered three dozen smelt.

"You must be from Astoria," observed the shopkeeper.

"How can you tell?" asked the old fisherman, "Because I ordered smelt?"

"No," replied the shopkeeper. "Because this is a hardware store."

*

What do Cannon Beach feminists smoke?
    Virginia Clams.

*

Why have Reedsport churches stopped christening babies?
    Few survived being hit in the head with a champagne bottle.

The Coast

An old man was sitting on the beach in Seaside when a seagull flew over and pooped on his head.

"Oh dear," said a woman who was passing by, "Let me get some toilet paper."

"Never mind," said the old man. "That bird is miles away by now."

*

A young Californian named Murph
After going to Newport to surf
Said, "The waves are a hoot
But without a wetsuit
I come out lookin' just like a Smurf."

*

What do you call two Oregon surfers in January?
Numb and Number.

Oregon's Best Jokes

What's adultery in Tillamook?
   Milking another man's cow.

*

What do Tillamook farmers use for relief of hemorrhoids?
   Preparation 4-H.

*

A tourist was hang gliding out near Cape Kiwanda. As he swooped over one of the local farms, two guys started shooting at him.
   "Did you see the size of that bird?" said the first one.
   "Sure did," replied the second one. "Too bad we missed him."
   "Oh well," shrugged the first one, "at least we made him drop that fella he was trying to carry off."

The Coast

What's the toughest part of being a Lincoln City yuppie?
    Deciding what wine goes with fishsticks.

*

A fisherman says to his friend, "I got a new pole for my wife."
    His friend says, "Good trade."

*

What do you get when you cross a spotted owl with a chinook salmon?
    100% unemployment in Coos Bay.

*

What does Daylight Savings Time mean on the coast?
    An extra hour of fog.

Eastern Oregon

*Where 'Dead End' is more than a road --
It's a way of life.*

A popular Pendleton doctor had his license revoked for improper conduct with a patient.

Two locals were discussing the problem when the first one said, "I think it's just inexcusable to have sex with your patients."

"I agree," said the second one, "but I'm still gonna miss him -- he was the best darn veterinarian we ever had."

Eastern Oregon

What is Pendleton's favorite TV show?
> Saturday Night Livestock!

*

What do they call calf roping in Pendleton?
> Foreplay.

*

What's the difference between I.Q. and temperature in La Grande?
> Sometimes the temperature gets over 100.

*

What's the best time to view the harvest moon in Eastern Oregon?
> When a wheat farmer bends over to fix his tractor.

Oregon's Best Jokes

A California tourist was driving through Eastern Oregon when he saw a farmer in the field pulling on a calf's leg that was coming out of a pregnant cow.

Even though he'd never been on a farm before, he stopped to offer some assistance.

After the calf was delivered, the farmer thanked the man profusely and then added, "If there's ever anything I can do for you, mister, let me know."

"Well, there is one thing," replied the tourist.

"What's that?" asked the farmer.

"Maybe you could tell me," said the Californian, scratching his head, "just how fast was the calf going when he hit that cow's ass?"

Eastern Oregon

What do you call a guy from Burns with 1500 girlfriends?
   A shepherd.

*

What's his favorite drink?
   Harvey Woolbanger.

*

What do Bend yuppies drive?
   A Mercedes with a winch.

Oregon's Best Jokes

What's long and hard on a guy from The Dalles?
    The third grade.

*

In Prineville, what is the difference between a bank and a family tree?
    A bank usually has several branches.

*

What does 501 stand for?
    The collective I.Q. of Eastern Oregon.

*

Did you hear about the guy from Klamath Falls who was killed during a pie eating contest?
    A cow stepped on his head.

Eastern Oregon

Why don't they play rap music in Hermiston?
> People keep trying to Square Dance to it.

*

What's the difference between a Pickup and a pair of Levi's?
> You can only fit one asshole into a pair of Levi's.

*

How does an Oregon wheat farmer know his girlfriend's dumped him?
> He gets a John Deere letter.

*

What's the nicest thing about living in Eastern Oregon?
> At least it's not Idaho.

Outdoor Life

*Come for the scenery.
Stay for the abuse.*

How can you spot the first-time tourist in Oregon?

> He's the one drinking Folgers Coffee in a styrofoam cup while trying to pump his own gas.

*

How can you spot the guy from the Oregon Visitors' Association?

> He's the one giving the tourist the wrong directions.

Outdoor Life

A sasquatch walks into a bar and orders a shot of whiskey.

The bartender pours the drink and charges him five dollars.

"You know," says the bartender, "We don't get many sasquatches in here."

"Yeah," says the sasquatch, "At these prices, I can understand why."

*

Where does Old MacDonald buy his camping equipment?
R-E-R-E-I.

*

Did you hear REI is selling a new rock climbing shoe designed by Midol?
Crampons.

Oregon's Best Jokes

"I prefer to think of it as urban camping."

What do you get when you cross a highway construction worker with an environmentalist?
A guy who wants to pave the whales.

*

What's big and white and extremely dangerous?
Mount N The Hood.

Outdoor Life

What is an Oregon pot grower's favorite song?
"Roll On, Columbian."

*

A bush pilot dropped off two elk hunters in a remote area near Sisters. When he returned, he found the hunters with two very large elk.

"You'll have to leave one of those behind," said the pilot. "It's too much weight for the plane. We'd never clear that mountain."

"What are you talking about?" asked the first hunter. "The pilot last year let us carry two elk."

"Okay," said the pilot, "but you'll have to leave some of your equipment behind."

"What are you talking about?"

Oregon's Best Jokes

asked the second hunter. "The pilot last year let us carry all our equipment."

"Okay," said the pilot. "If last year's pilot said it was okay, I guess we can do it."

They loaded up the elk and the equipment and took off. The small plane skimmed across the top of the trees as they approached the mountains.

Suddenly, there was a loud crash. When the men awoke, they pulled themselves from the wreakage.

"Where the heck are we?" asked the pilot as he staggered to his feet.

"I dunno," said the first hunter, "but from the looks of things, I'd say we're about a half mile further than last year."

Outdoor Life

One fisherman said to the other, "That Willamette River is polluted."
"How can you tell?"
"Last fish I caught -- I pulled him out of water, he thanked me."

*

What is the most dangerous invertebrate in the woods?
A .45 Caliber Slug.

*

What's the difference between a slug and a prune?
A dash of salt.

*

What do you get when you cross a slug with a centipede?
A Thousand Trails.

Oregon's Best Jokes

What's a slug's favorite soft drink?
    Slemon-slime.

*

Who leaves a trail of silver as he goes off into the sunset?
    The Lone Slug.

*

A guy was out deer hunting in the Cascades when he accidently shot his partner. The guy loaded him into their truck and rushed him to the hospital.

After the doctors finished their examination, he asked, "Is my friend going to make it?"

"Well," replied the physician, "he would have stood a better chance if you hadn't gutted him first."

Outdoor Life

Who were the first chicken farmers to explore the Willamette Valley?
Lewis and Cluck.

*

This teacher brings venison jerky to school and asks her students to guess what animal it came from.
"Cow," says Bobby.
"No, It's not cow," she says.
"Lamb," says Billy.
"No, it's not lamb."
"Pig," says Jennifer.
"No, it's not pig," says the teacher. "Why don't I give you a little hint. It's something that your mommy calls your daddy."
From the back of the room, Johnny yells, "Spit it out! Spit it out! It's asshole!"

Oregon Names

OREGON
Up a creek without a paddle.

ASTORIA
The red ring left on a person's backside after sitting too long on a toilet seat.

BLODGETT
The little baseball bat used by fishermen to render fish unconscious after pulling them into the boat.

Oregon Names

BUELL
A rather unpleasant ointment.

CALAPOOIA
That stain left in men's underpants even after they've been washed.

CHITWOOD
The brown plastic veneer on cheap stereo speakers painted to resemble wood.

CLACKAMAS
The sound your car makes when it needs a tune-up.

CLARNO
Anyone over the age of eighteen who still hangs his buns out of a car window.

Oregon's Best Jokes

CLATSOP
Those little scissors used for trimming nose hairs.

DESCHUTES
A condition caused by too much Mexican food.

GRAND RONDE
A turd that is too large to be flushed down the toilet.

IDLEYLD
That maze of ropes at the bank that gives you the impression that you're standing in line for a ride at Disneyland.

IRRIGON
The nozzles on a milking machine.

Oregon Names

KAH-NEE-TA
Indian expression meaning "Kah-See-No."

LAURELHURST
Any Rose Parade float sponsored by a funeral home.

Oregon's Best Jokes

MALHEUR
The smell on someone's breath after eating a bag of Doritos.

MOLALLA
The stream of saliva that clings to your lip after a shot of novocaine.

MONMOUTH
A disease caused by having intercourse with livestock.

MULTNOMAH
An abnormally large mole usually with a hair growing out of it.

NESTUCCA
The folds of skin on fat people that collect foreign particles while lying in the sun.

Oregon Names

NETARTS
The little reflective bumps on the center line of most highways.

NIMROD
A person who wears adult diapers under a pair of tight jeans.

OCHOCO
The peculiar odor that emanates from a pulp mill.

OSWEGO
The liquid that collects in your bellybutton while sunbathing.

OWYHEE
A condition caused when one's genitals are exposed to extremely cold water.

Oregon's Best Jokes

PEDEE
The little dab of liquid that, no matter how long you shake it, still runs down your leg.

PEORIA
The warm spot left in a swimming pool after someone has just urinated.

PROVOLT
A positively charged electrical ion.

SCAPPOOSE
Any foreign substance found underneath a table or countertop.

SILETZ
The stuff that comes out of a slug after you pour salt on it.

Oregon Names

SILTCOOS
That weird looking skin that forms on day-old cocoa or soup.

SISKIYOU
An old Indian expression for "one who skips during war dances."

TAHKENITCH
Spot on a dog that, when scratched, makes its leg jerk uncontrollably.

TERREBONNE
The metal crossbar on a boy's bike that causes excruciating pain when you slip off the seat and land on it.

TUMALO
The vertical crease on a woman's abdomen from wearing pantyhose.

Oregon's Best Jokes

UMPQUA
What's left of an animal after it's been run over by a Mack truck.

WALLOWA
The lopsided wheel found on grocery carts that causes them to drive erratically.

WEDDERBURN
A persistent itch from swimming in the Willamette River.

WINLOCK
A psychological condition that keeps the Trailblazers from becoming NBA Champions.

The End

Cruising down Highway 101